and annoying
GROSS SONGS
Kids Love To Sing!

BY: KEN CARDER

ILLUSTRATIONS: TAMMY ORTNER

www.twinsisters.com
1-800-248-TWIN (8946)
Twin Sisters Productions, LLC • Akron, OH

Credits:
Publisher: Twin Sisters Productions, LLC
Executive Producers: Kim Mitzo Thompson, Karen Mitzo Hilderbrand
Music Arranged by: Hal Wright
Workbook Author: Ken Carder
Book Design: Angelee Randlett, Christine Della Penna
Illustrations: Tammy Ortner

ISBN 1575838214

About the Author

KEN CARDER

Ken is a graduate of The University of Akron in Akron, OH with a B.A. in Communication And Rhetoric, and of Evangelical School of Theology in Myerstown, PA with a M.Div. For the past three years Ken has worked exclusively with Twin Sisters Productions to develop new educational music resources for children. Ken is the Children's Pastor at Community Church of Portage Lakes (Akron, OH). He and his wife have worked extensively with young children in churches, summer camps, schools, a syndicated radio ministry broadcast, and community theater. Ken and his wife are proud parents of three children, Stephen, Nathan, and McKenna.

TABLE OF CONTENTS

Gross *and annoying* Songs Kids Love To Sing

"ROAD KILL STEW! ROAD KILL STEW.
TASTES SO GOOD, JUST LIKE IT SHOULD."

 = Adult Help Recommended

INTRODUCTION

Most kids love the chance to be gross and disgusting. I've reached that conclusion after many years of summer camp ministries with children and middle-school kids. The opportunity to say or do something gross and revolting brings a freedom from kids' often boring days and predictable routines. It's exhilarating to do something you wouldn't normally do—and not be punished for it!

Enjoy the Gross and Not-So-Gross Songs at home, while on vacation, around a cozy family campfire or a not-so-cozy bonfire at the end of a day at summer camp! You'll be surprised how kids will laugh, groan, and sing along. Lead the singing with a simple guitar. Don't worry about how bad you think you might sound—few kids or adults will sound any better. Just concentrate on creating a memory or two for kids! Make up additional verses or change a few words to customize the songs to your group experiences. The bottom line… have fun!

Toss out a few jokes and riddles between songs—the kids will groan and maybe beg you to stop. But the truth is they're smiling inside, begging you for more, and can't wait to tell the same joke to someone else!

Play Together! Some adults have concluded that kids today don't know how to have fun apart from their video games and competitive sports. Try a few of the large group field activities, the thinking games, the gross competitions, the stunts and experiments. Get kids up, moving, laughing, and playing together.

The Gross and Not-so-Gross Things To Make are ideas of easy crafts to do at home or camp. These are perfect for a rainy day, that downtime during the afternoon. Keep in mind that it's not the quality of the crafts that matter most. What matters is the interaction and relationship building—the memories that are being made. Most kids love Skits and Pranks. I've included some very old classic sketches and practical jokes that kids can do with very little rehearsal. A few of the puns might need to be explained…you'll know by the looks on the audience faces.

Gross Food—this is where most of the adults will bail out! I've selected recipes that might tug at your stomach and will certainly get a reaction from kids of all ages. A word of advice: don't try them all at the same time!

Caution: some of the games, activities, and recipes will need some adult supervision.
Look for this symbol:

Finally, for our younger kids, we've included Greasy Grimy Gopher Guts—the Game. The kids will have great fun playing variations of classic card games with this unusual deck of cards.

May you have a disgustingly beautiful time together with the kids you love! Remember, have fun and create a memory.

Kon Cardor

GREASY GRIMY GOPHER GUTS

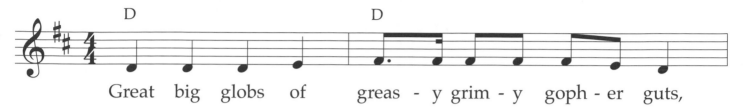

Great big globs of greas - y grim - y goph - er guts,

ju - bi-la - ted mon-key's meat, con - cen-tra-ted bird - ies feet, a

great big jar of all pur - pose por - poise pus, and

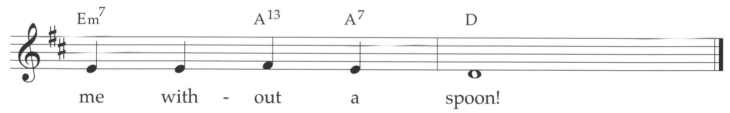

me with - out a spoon!

NOBODY LIKES ME

No - bod-y likes me, ev-'ry-bod-y hates me, think I'll go eat worms,

big fat juic-y ones, een-y ween-y squeem-y ones, see how they wig-gle and squirm.

ON TOP OF MY PIZZA

On top of my piz - za, _____ all cov - ered with sauce, _____ could not find the mush - rooms, _____ I think they got lost. _____ I looked in the clo - set, _____ I looked in the sink, _____ I looked in the cup that _____ held my co - la drink.

2.
I looked in the saucepan, right under the lid.
No matter where I looked, those mushrooms stayed hid.
Next time you make pizza, I'm begging you, please,
Do not give me mushrooms, but just plain old cheese.

MICHAEL FINNEGAN

There once was a man named Mi - chael Fin - ne - gan.

He grew wis - kers on his chin - ne - gan. The

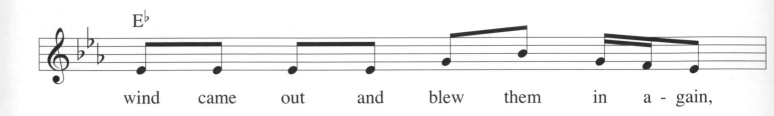

wind came out and blew them in a - gain,

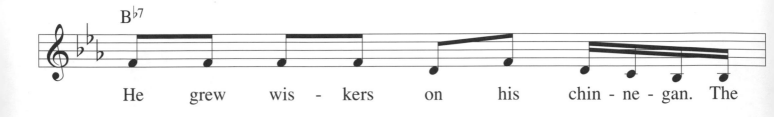

poor old Mi - chael Fin - ne - gan, be - gin a - gain!

2.
There once was a man named Michael Finnegan.
He went fishing with a pinnegan.
Caught a fish but he dropped it in again.
Poor old Michael Finnegan, begin again!

3.
There once was a man named Michael Finnegan.
Climbed a tree and barked his shinnigan.
Took off several yards of skinnigan.
Poor old Michael Finnegan, begin again!

4.
There once was a man named Michael Finnegan.
He grew fat and he grew thin again.
Then he died and we have to begin again.
Poor old Michael Finnegan, begin again!

OH, TOM THE TOAD

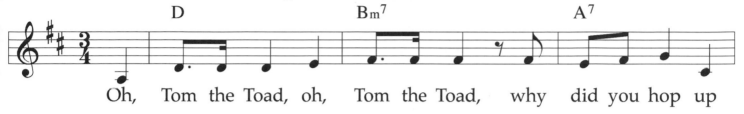

Oh, Tom the Toad, oh, Tom the Toad, why did you hop up

on the road? Oh, Tom the Toad, oh, Tom the Toad, why

did you hop up on the road? You were my friend, and

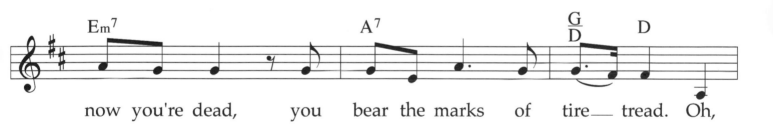

now you're dead, you bear the marks of tire— tread. Oh,

Tom the Toad, oh, Tom the Toad, why did you hop up on the road?

2.
O Tom the toad, O Tom the toad
Why did you hop up on the road?
O Tom the toad, O Tom the toad
Why did you hop up on the road?

You did not see yon passing car
And now you're stretched out on the tar
O Tom the Toad, O Tom the Toad
Why did you hop up on the road?

TAKE IT OUT, REMOVE IT

Oh, I stuck my head in a lit-tle skunk's hole, the

lit-tle skunk said, "Up-on my soul,— take it out, take it out, take it

out, re - move it!" Oh, I out, re - move it!" Well, I

did - n't take it out— and the lit-tle skunk said, "If you

don't take it out you will wish that you were dead, take it

out, take it out, PSSSSST! I re - moved it!

SWITCH

I don't care if I go cra-zy, 1, 2, 3, 4, 5, 6, Switch!

Cra-zy go I, if care don't I, 6, 5, 4, 3, 2, 1, Switch!

THERE WAS A LITTLE ROOSTER

Oh, there was a lit-tle roos-ter in our lit-tle coun-try store, and he

phfft! on the count-ter and he phfft! on the floor, and he

phfft! on the su-gar and he phfft! on the bread, and if

I had-n't ducked he'd have phfft! on my head.

THE BEAR WENT OVER THE MOUNTAIN

The bear went o-ver the moun-tain, the bear went o-ver the

moun-tain, the bear went o-ver the moun-tain to see what he could

see.___ To see what he could see,___ to see what he could

see.___ The bear went o-ver the moun-tain, the bear went o-ver the

moun-tain, the bear went o-ver the moun-tain to see what he could see.

2.
The other side of the mountain,
The other side of the mountain,
The other side of the mountain,
Was all that he could see.

Was all that he could see,
Was all that he could see.
The other side of the mountain,
The other side of the mountain,
The other side of the mountain,
Was all that he could see.

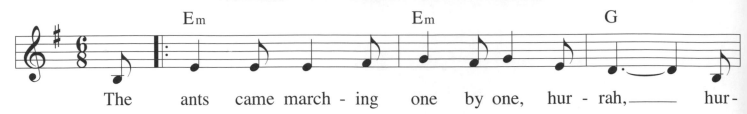

THE ANTS CAME MARCHING

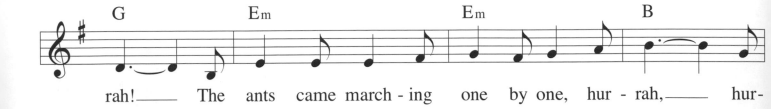

The ants came march - ing one by one, hur - rah,_____ hur-

rah!_____ The ants came march - ing one by one, hur - rah,_____ hur-

rah!_____ The ants came march_____ing one by one, the lit-tle one stopped to

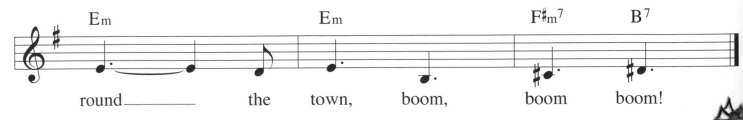

suck his thumb and they all go march ing down_____ a-

round_____ the town, boom, boom boom!

The ants came marching two by two, hurrah, hurrah …
The little one stopped to tie his shoe…

The ants came marching three by three, hurrah, hurrah …
The little one stopped to climb a tree …

The ants came marching four by four, hurrah, hurrah …
The little one stopped to shut the door…

The ants came marching five by five, hurrah, hurrah …
The little one stopped to take a dive …

The ants came marching six by six, hurrah, hurrah …
The little one stopped to pick up sticks…

The ants came marching seven by seven, hurrah, hurrah…
The little one stopped to go to heaven…

The ants came marching eight by eight, hurrah, hurrah…
The little one stopped to shut the gate…

The ants came marching nine by nine, hurrah, hurrah…
The little one stopped to scratch his spine…

The ants came marching ten by ten,
hurrah, hurrah…
The little one stopped to say
        "THE END"…

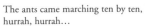

ROAD KILL STEW

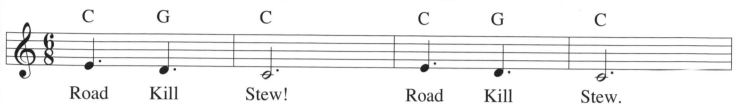

Road   Kill   Stew!   Road   Kill   Stew.

*May be sung as a round beginning here.

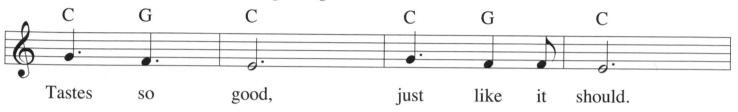

Tastes   so   good,   just   like   it   should.

First you go down to the   In - ter-state, you   wait for the crit -ter to

meet   its fate. You take   it home and you   make it great!

Road   Kill   Stew.   Road   Kill   Stew.

THE CAT CAME BACK

Well, old Mis-ter John-son had trou-bles all his own, he had an

old yel-low cat that wouldn't leave home. Tried

ev - 'ry-thing he knew to get the cat to stay a - way, e - ven

took him up to Can - a - da and told him for to stay, but the

cat came back the ver - y next day, they

thought he was a gon - er but the cat came back 'cause he

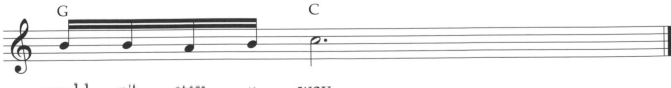

would - n't stay a - way.

2.
Well they gave a boy a dollar for to set the cat afloat
And he took him up the river in a sack and a boat.
Now the fishing, it was fine until the news got around
That the boat was missing and the boy was drowned.

But the cat came back the very next day,
They thought he was a goner
   but the cat came back
   'cause he wouldn't stay away.

3.
Well, the farmer on the corner said he'd shoot him on sight
And he loaded up his gun full of rocks and dynamite.
The gun went off, heard all over town.
Little pieces of the man was all that they found

But the cat came back the very next day,
They thought he was a goner
   but the cat came back
   'cause he wouldn't stay away.

4.
Now they gave him to a man going up in a balloon
And they told him for to leave him with the man in the moon.
The balloon it busted, back to earth did head.
Seven miles away they picked the man up dead.

But the cat came back the very next day,
They thought he was a goner
   but the cat came back
   'cause he wouldn't stay away.

5.
Well; they finally found a way this cat for to fix.
They put him in an orange crate on Route 66.
Come a ten-ton truck with a 20-ton load,
Scattered pieces of the orange crate all down the road.

But the cat came back the very next day,
They thought he was a goner
   but the cat came back
   'cause he wouldn't stay away.

6.
Well, they took him to the shop where the meat was ground,
And they dropped him in the hopper when the butcher wasn't 'round.
Well, the cat disappeared with a blood-curdling shriek
And the town's meat tasted furry for a week.

But the cat came back the very next day,
They thought he was a goner
   but the cat came back
   'cause he wouldn't stay away.

7.
And from Cape Canaveral they put him into place,
Shot him in a rocket going way out in space.
They finally thought the cat was out of human reach.
Next day they got a call from Miami Beach.

But the cat came back the very next day,
They thought he was a goner
   but the cat came back
   'cause he wouldn't stay away.

GROSS SONGS

and annoying Gross Songs kids love to sing!

TWO LITTLE FLEAS

Two lit - tle fleas to - geth - er sat, they___ cried when one flea said, "I've had no place to lay my head, since___ my old dog is dead. I've

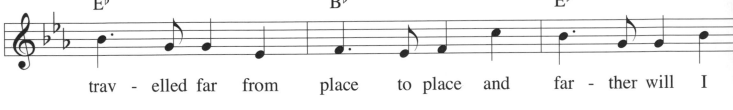

trav - elled far from place to place and far - ther will I roam, but the next old dog that shows his face will___

be my home sweet home."

MARY HAD A SWARM OF BEES

C   Am⁷   Dm⁷   G¹³

Mar - y had a swarm of bees,   swarm of bees,   swarm of bees,

C   Am⁷   G⁷   C

Mar - y had a swarm of bees and   they to save their lives...

C   Am⁷   Dm⁷   G¹³

had   to go where Mar - y went,   Mar - y went,   Mar - y went,

C   Am⁷   G⁷   C

had   to go where Mar - y went 'cause   Mar - y had the hives.

I'M A NUT

I'm a lit-tle a-corn, nice and round, I live a-way down

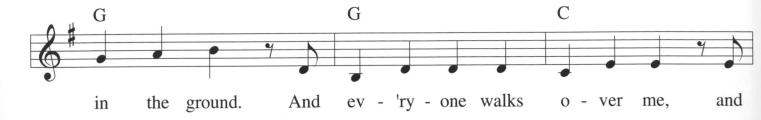

in the ground. And ev-'ry-one walks o-ver me, and

Click with tongue

that is why I'm cracked you see. I'm a nut, *(click, click)* in a

rut! *(click, click)* I'm a nut, *(click, click)* in a rut! *(click, click)*

YON YONSON

My name is Yon Yon - son, I came from Wis -

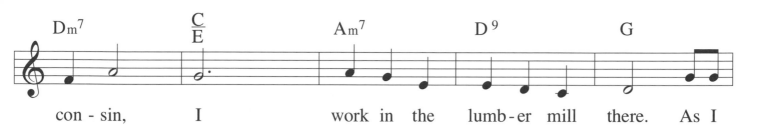

con - sin, I work in the lumb -er mill there. As I

walk down the street___ all the peo - ple I meet___

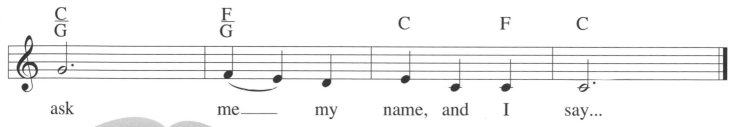

ask me___ my name, and I say...

SQUIRTY ORANGE

F   C   (spoken)

Oh, I wish I were a lit-tle squir-ty orange, squir-ty orange, oh, I

C   F   (spoken)

wish I were a lit-tle squir-ty orange, squir-ty orange, I'd go

B♭   A⁷   Dm

squir-ty squir-ty squir-ty o-ver ev-'ry-bo-dy's shir-ty, oh, I

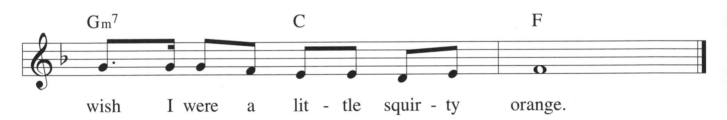

Gm⁷   C   F

wish I were a lit-tle squir-ty orange.

Oh, I wish I were a little bottle of pop (bottle of pop)
Oh, I wish I were a little bottle of pop (bottle of pop)
I'd go down with a slurp and come up with a burp
Oh, I wish I were a little bottle of pop (bottle of pop)

Oh, I wish I were a little foreign car (foreign car)
Oh, I wish I were a little foreign car (foreign car)
I'd go speedy, speedy, speedy over everybody's feety
Oh, I wish I were a little foreign car (foreign car)

Oh, I wish I were a little mosquito (mosquito)
Oh, I wish I were a little mosquito (mosquito)
I'd go hidey, hidey, hidey under everybody's nightie
Oh, I wish I were a little mosquito (mosquito)

Oh, I wish I were a little band-aid (band-aid)
Oh, I wish I were a little band-aid (band-aid)
I'd stick to the hairs and pull them up in pairs
Oh, I wish I were a little band-aid (band-aid)

Oh, I wish I were a little striped skunk (striped skunk)
Oh, I wish I were a little striped skunk (striped skunk)
I'd sit up in the trees and perfume all the breeze
Oh, I wish I were a little striped skunk (striped skunk)

RAVIOLI

Rav - i - o - li, I like rav - i - o - li, rav - i - o - li,

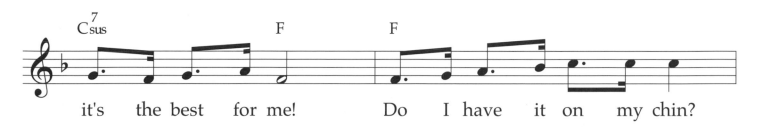

it's the best for me! Do I have it on my chin?

Yes, you've got it on your chin! On my chin? On your chin!

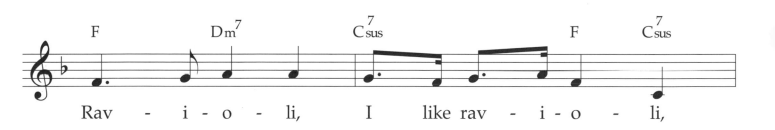

Rav - i - o - li, I like rav - i - o - li,

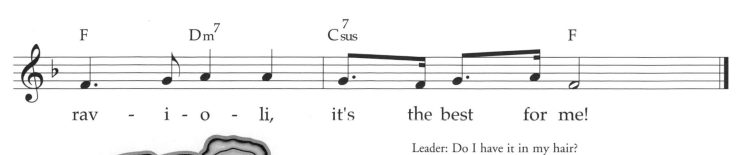

rav - i - o - li, it's the best for me!

Leader: Do I have it in my hair?
Everyone: Yes, you've got it in your hair! …

Leader: Do I have it in my ears?
Everyone: Yes, you've got in your ears! …

LITTLE BLACK THINGS

Lit - tle black things, lit - tle black things, run - ning

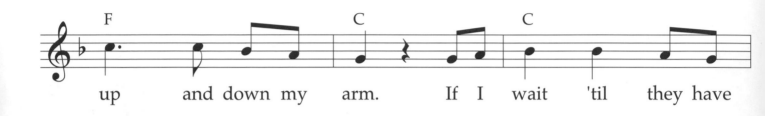

up and down my arm. If I wait 'til they have

ba - bies I can start a black thing farm.

2.
Haven't had a bath in two years
And I never wash my clothes
'Cause I got these little black things
Where they came from no one knows
Chorus

3.
Had a boyfriend, tried to kiss me
But he turned and gave a yell
And I never got to ask him
Was it the black things or the smell?
Chorus

THE BABY BUMBLEBEE

Oh I'm bring-ing home a ba - by bum - ble bee.

Won't my mom-my be so proud of me, 'cause I'm bring-ing home a ba-by

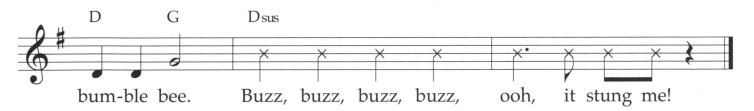

bum-ble bee. Buzz, buzz, buzz, buzz, ooh, it stung me!

2.
Oh, I'm bringing home a baby rattlesnake
Won't my mommy shiver and shake
'Cause I'm bringing home a baby rattlesnake
Rattle, rattle, rattle
OOOOH, it bit me!

3.
Oh, I'm bringing home a baby dinosaur
Won't my mommy fall right through the floor
'Cause I'm bringing home a baby dinosaur
Gobble, gobble, gobble
OOOOH, it ate me!

THERE'S A HOLE IN THE BUCKET

There's a hole in the buck-et,—— dear Li - za, dear

Li-za, there's a hole in the buck-et,—— dear Li - za a hole!

Then fix it, dear Henry
Dear Henry, dear Henry
Then fix it, dear Henry
Dear Henry, fix it!

With what shall I fix it
Dear Liza, dear Liza
With what shall I fix it
Dear Liza, with what?

With a straw, dear Henry
Dear Henry, dear Henry
With a straw, dear Henry
Dear Henry, a straw!

But the straw is too long
Dear Liza, dear Liza
But the straw is too long
Dear Liza, too long!

Then cut it, dear Henry
Dear Henry, dear Henry
Then cut it, dear Henry
Dear Henry, cut it!

With what shall I cut it
Dear Liza, dear Liza
With what shall I cut it
Dear Liza, with what?

With an axe, dear Henry
Dear Henry, dear Henry
With an axe, dear Henry
Dear Henry, an axe!

The axe is too dull
Dear Liza, dear Liza
The axe is too dull
Dear Liza, too dull!

Then sharpen it, dear Henry
Dear Henry, dear Henry
Then sharpen it, dear Henry
Dear Henry, sharpen it!

With what shall I sharpen it
Dear Liza, dear Liza
With what shall I sharpen it
Dear Liza, with what?

With a stone, dear Henry
Dear Henry, dear Henry
With a stone, dear Henry
Dear Henry, a stone!

The stone is too dry
Dear Liza, dear Liza
The stone is too dry
Dear Liza, too dry!

Then wet it, dear Henry
Dear Henry, dear Henry
Then wet it, dear Henry
Dear Henry, wet it!

With what shall I wet it
Dear Liza, dear Liza
With what shall I wet it
Dear Liza, with what?

With water, dear Henry
Dear Henry, dear Henry
With water, dear Henry
Dear Henry, water!

How shall I get it
Dear Liza, dear Liza
How shall I get it
Dear Liza, get it?

In the bucket, dear Henry
Dear Henry, dear Henry
In the bucket, dear Henry
Dear Henry, the bucket!

There's a hole in the bucket
Dear Liza, dear Liza
There's a hole in the bucket
Dear Liza, a hole!

Then fix it, dear Henry
Dear Henry, dear Henry
Then fix it, dear Henry
Dear Henry, fix it!

NERO, MY DOG, HAS FLEAS

HAVE YOU EVER SEEN?

Have you ev - er seen a horse fly, a

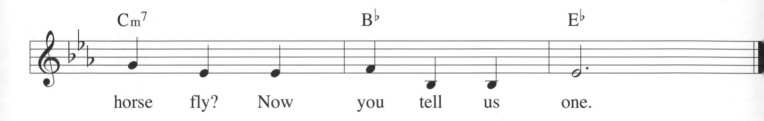

horse fly, a horse fly? Have you ev - er seen a

horse fly? Now you tell us one.

2.
Have you ever seen a shoe box, a shoe box,
a shoe box? …

3.
Have you ever seen a chimney sweep, a chimney sweep,
a chimney sweep? …

4.
Have you ever seen a dish mop, a dish mop,
a dish mop? …

THE GREEN GRASS GREW ALL AROUND

Oh, in the woods there was a tree, the

pret-ti-est lit - tle tree that you ev - er did see. And the

tree was in the ground, and the green grass grew all a -

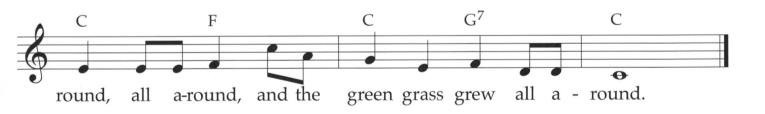

round, all a-round, and the green grass grew all a - round.

2.
And on this tree there was a limb,
The prettiest littlest limb that you ever did see
And the tree was in the ground
And the green grass grew all around, all around
And the green grass grew all around

3.
And on this limb there was a branch
The prettiest littlest branch that you ever did see
And the branch was on the tree
And the tree was in the ground
And the green grass grew all around, all around
And the green grass grew all around

4.
And on this branch there was a twig
The prettiest littlest twig that you ever did see
And the twig was on the branch
And the branch was on the tree
And the tree was in the ground
And the green grass grew all around, all around
And the green grass grew all around

5.
And on this twig there was a leaf
The prettiest littlest leaf that you ever did see
And the leaf was on the twig
And the twig was on the branch

And the branch was on the tree
And the tree was in the ground
And the green grass grew all around, all around
And the green grass grew all around

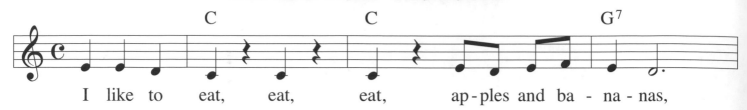

APPLES AND BANANAS

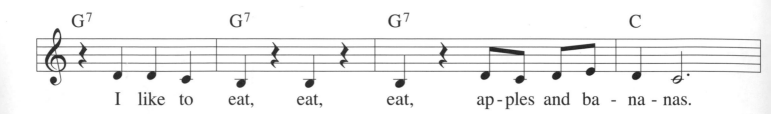

I like to eat, eat, eat, ap-ples and ba - na - nas,

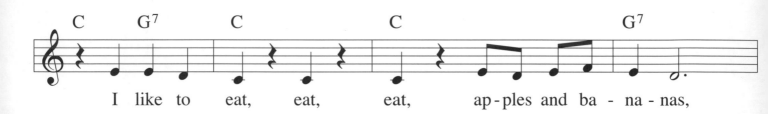

I like to eat, eat, eat, ap-ples and ba - na - nas.

I like to eat, eat, eat, ap-ples and ba - na - nas,

I like to eat, eat, eat, ap-ples and ba - na - nas.

2. I like to ate, ate, ate ay-ples and ba-nay-nays…

3. I like to eat, eat, eat ee-ples and bee-nee-nees…

4. I like to ite, ite, ite i-ples and bi-ni-nies…

5. I like to ote, ote, ote oh-ples and bo-no-nos…

6. I like to oot, oot, oot oo-ples and boo-noo-noos…

BLACK SOCKS

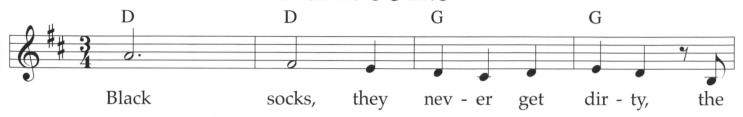

D   D   G   G

Black   socks,   they   nev - er   get   dir - ty,   the

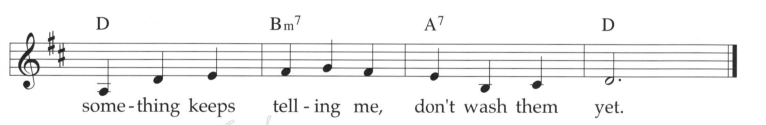

D   B m7   E7   A

long - er   you   wear them the   strong - er   they   get.

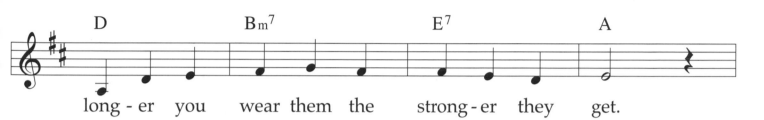

D   D   G   G

Some - - - - times   I   think of the   laun - dry,   but

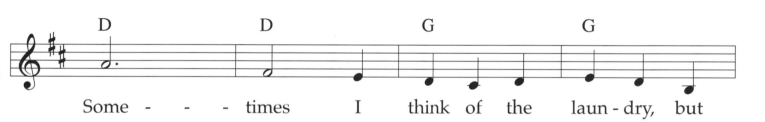

D   B m7   A7   D

some - thing keeps   tell - ing me,   don't wash them   yet.

BRING BACK MY NEIGHBORS TO ME

Last night as I lay on my pil - low,_____ last

night as I lay on my bed,_____ I stuck my feet out the

win - dow,_____ in the morn - ing my neigh - bors were dead.

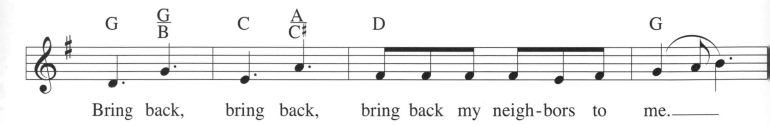

Bring back, bring back, bring back my neigh - bors to me._____

Bring back, bring back, bring back my neigh - bors to me.

EVERYWHERE THAT WE GO

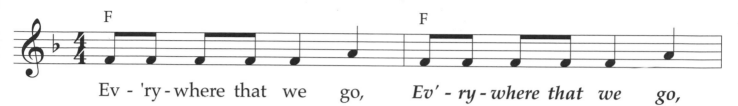

Ev - 'ry - where that we go, Ev' - ry - where that we go,

peo - ple al - ways ask us peo - ple al - ways ask us

who we are_____ who we are_____ and

where do we come from. and where do we come from.

So we tell them, So we tell them,

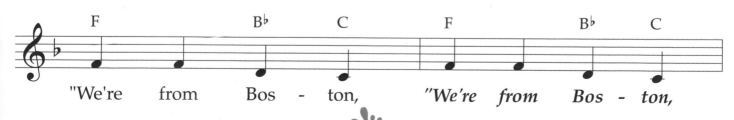

"We're from Bos - ton, "We're from Bos - ton,

might-y might-y Bos - ton!" *might-y might-y Bos - ton!"* And

if they can't hear us, *And if they can't hear us* we

sing a lit - tle loud - er. *we sing a lit - tle loud - er.*

2.
...We're from London (We're from London)
Mighty, mighty London (Mighty, mighty London)…

3.
...We're from Rio (We're from Rio)
Mighty, mighty Rio (Mighty, mighty Rio)…

4.
...We're from Paris (We're from Paris)
Mighty, mighty Paris (Mighty, mighty Paris)…

5.
...We're from Hong Kong (We're from Hong Kong)
Mighty, mighty Hong Kong (Mighty, mighty Hong Kong)…

6.
...We're from Sydney (We're from Sydney)
Mighty, mighty Sydney (Mighty, mighty Sydney)

And if they can't hear us —they're deaf!

Groaners
Jokes Kids Love To Tell

1.
Why did the toilet paper roll down the hill?
Because it wanted to get to the bottom!

2.
How do you make a snake cry?
Take away its rattle!

3.
What monkey can fly?
A hot air baboon!

4.
What happened to the mouse who fell into a glass of soda?
Nothing, it was a soft drink!

5.
Why did the firefly get bad grades in school?
He wasn't very bright!

6.
Why do birds fly south?
It's too far to walk!

7.
Why did the boy bring toilet paper to the birthday party?
Because he's a party pooper!

8.
What's worse than finding a worm in your apple?
Finding half a worm!

9.
What is a dog's favorite snack?
Pupcorn

10.
Why don't elephants pick their nose?
They don't know where to hide a 30-pound booger!

11.
Why did the booger cross the road?
Because he was tired of getting picked on.

12.
How do you count cows?
With a cowculator!

13.
Why did the fish cross the river?
To get to its school!

14.
What did the chicken say to the farmer?
Nothing! A chicken can't talk!

15.
What is a volcano?
A mountain with hiccups!

16.
Why does a hummingbird hum?
It doesn't know the words!

17.
Why does a gorilla have big nostrils?
Because it has big fingers!

18.
Why didn't the skeleton cross the road?
Because he had no body to go with!

19.
Where do you find a dog with no legs?
Right where you left him!

20.
What is Beethoven doing in his grave?
Decomposing!

21.
What do you call two spiders who just got married?
Newlywebs!

22.
What does a crab use to call someone?
A shellular phone!

23.
What is the difference between boogers & broccoli?
Kids don't eat broccoli

24.
What do rabbits do when they get married?
Go on a bunnymoon

25.
How do you make a tissue dance?
Put a little boogie in it!

26.
Why did the chicken cross the playground?
To get to the other slide.

27.
What do you call a sleeping bull?
A bulldozer!

28.
My friend is built upside down...
His nose runs, and his feet smell!

29.
What is the best thing to take into the desert?
A thirst aid kit!

30.
What do you call a fish without an eye?
A Fsh!

31.
What is black and white, black and white, and green?
Two skunks fighting over a pickle!

32.
How do birds get in shape?
They do worm-ups!

33.
Where does a spider look for new words?
In the Webster's dictionary

34.
If everyone in the country drove a pink automobile, what would we be?
A pink carnation!

35.
Which side of the chicken do the feathers grow on?
The outside!

36.
What did the snake give to his girlfriend on their first date?
A good night hiss!

37.
Doctor, Doctor... What did the x-ray of my head show?
Nothing.

38.
What do you call a monkey holding a firecracker?
A baboom!

39.
What did one firefly say to the other before he left?
Bye! I'm glowing now!

40.
Doctor, Doctor... did you hear about the boy who swallowed a quarter?
There's no change yet.

41.
What did the cat eat for breakfast?
Mice Crispies

42.
Why was the father centipede so upset?
All of the kids needed new shoes!

43.
What did the dog say when he sat on sandpaper?
Rufffff

44.
What do you call a pony with a sore throat?
A little horse!

45.
What pet makes the loudest noise?
A trum-pet!

39

46.
What did the teddy bear say when the monkey
offered him dessert?
No thanks, I'm stuffed.

47.
How do bees travel?
They take the buzz!

48.
How does a dog smell?
Badly!

49.
Why are frogs good outfielders?
Because they can catch lots of flies.

50.
How do you make a witch itch?
Take away her W.

51.
Why did the gum cross the road?
Because it was stuck to the chicken's foot!

52.
Why did the tomato blush?
Because it saw the salad dressing!

53.
What does a dentist call his x-rays?
Tooth-pics!

54.
What do you get when you cross a
bird, a car, and a dog?
A flying car-pet

55.
How come a cheetah can't play hide and seek?
Because he's already been spotted.

56.
What has four wheels and flies?
A garbage truck!

57.
Why did the turkey cross the road?
To prove that he wasn't chicken!

58.
What invention enables man to walk through walls?
A door.

59.
What did the math book say to the other math book?
"I've got problems."

60.
Where do snowmen go to dance?
A snowball!

Experiments & Stunts

BACKYARD VOLCANO

No need to visit Mount St. Helens or the island of Hawaii to see a volcano! Make your own.

You'll need:

- A small mound of dirt outside
- An empty 35mm film canister
- Baking soda
- Red or yellow food coloring (optional)
- Vinegar
- Liquid dish washing soap

Outside, make a mound of dirt—size really doesn't matter so don't knock yourself out! Put the film canister into the top of your volcano. Pour two spoonfuls of baking soda and one spoonful of soap in the film canister. For a cool effect, add a few drops of the red or yellow food coloring. When you're ready, add about an ounce of the vinegar into the container! Watch what happens.

FAKE WOUNDS

Bring out a scream with one or more fake wounds and a great story!

You'll need:

- Petroleum jelly
- Toothpick
- Bowl
- Red food coloring
- A white tissue
- Powdered cocoa

Place a finger-full of petroleum jelly into a bowl. Use a toothpick to blend three or four drops of red food coloring with the petroleum jelly. To make the color a darker bloodlike red, blend in a pinch of cocoa. Separate the layers of a facial tissue, then rip out a small rectangle from one layer about 3 inches by 2 inches. Place the tissue at your wound site (the back of the forearm is a good spot). First, cover the tissue with the plain petroleum jelly, molding a gooey wound. Smear the blood-colored petroleum jelly in the center of the wound, sprinkle cocoa onto the edges, and rub the cocoa in to make the edges dark. Now go show someone! Be prepared with a sad tale or spine-tingling story, too!

NATURAL GAS

Wow your friends by inflating a balloon using natural gas! It's not what you're thinking!

You'll need:

- One packet of yeast (available in the grocery store)
- A small, clean, clear, plastic soda bottle
- 1 teaspoon of sugar
- Warm water
- Small balloon

Fill the bottle with about one inch of warm water. Add all of the yeast and gently swirl the bottle a few seconds. Add the sugar and swirl it around some more. As the yeast absorbs the sugar, it creates a GAS—carbon dioxide. Put the neck of the balloon over the top of the bottle and allow the bottle to sit for awhile in a warm place. Soon the balloon should start to blow up because it is filling with the gas created by the living yeast! When you've amazed your friends, remove the balloon and throw it away. Pour out the yeast solution in the sink. What does it smell like?

STALK SHOW

You'll need:

- Celery stalk or white cut flowers
- Red food coloring
- Tall, clear jar
- Water

Pour water in a tall, clear jar and add the red food coloring. Stand a stalk of celery in the glass. Wait 24 hours, and the celery leaves will turn red. This will work, too, with white flowers. In a process called osmosis, the plants absorb the water—and the coloring—and carry it to the leaves.

CLOUDY DAY

Make your own clouds!

You'll need:
- Metal cake pan
- Ice cubes
- Glass jar
- Hot water

Fill a metal cake pan with ice and wait a few minutes for the pan to cool. Carefully pour two inches of hot tap water into a wide-mouthed glass jar. Set the pan of ice on the jar rim and watch what happens. The water in the jar will evaporate, causing vapor to fill the jar. As it nears the air at the top, the vapor will cool and condense on the sides of the jar and the bottom of the pan. In the same way, clouds form in the sky when water vapor condenses on particles of dust or salt. Rain falls when water droplets in the cloud become too heavy to stay aloft.

PAPER CLIP FLOAT

Don't eat or drink this float—hold out for the rootbeer float from your favorite ice cream hangout. But challenge your friends to make a paper clip float!

You'll need:
- Clean, dry paper clips
- Toilet tissue paper
- A bowl of water
- Pencil with eraser

Fill the bowl with water, and place a paper clip on top of the water. The paper clip will sink. Let others try, then gently drop one sheet of toilet tissue paper flat onto the surface of the water. Now, carefully place a dry paper clip flat on top of the tissue. Use the eraser end of the pencil to carefully poke the tissue—not the paper clip—until the tissue sinks. With some luck, the tissue will sink and leave the paper clip floating!

LAVA LIGHT

You'll need:

- Glass jar
- Water
- Food coloring
- Vegetable oil
- Salt

Fill a glass jar with about 3 inches of water and add food coloring. Add 1/3 cup of vegetable oil and wait until the layers settle. Shake salt into the jar while you count to five. The oil and salt should form a glob and sink to the bottom of the jar. As the salt dissolves in the water, the oil should float back to the top. Keep adding more salt to watch the action repeat.

At first, the oil floats on the water because it's less dense than the water and doesn't mix with water. When you shake salt onto the oil, the salt clings to the oil and drags a glob to the bottom. In time, however, the salt starts to dissolve in the water until it can no longer hold down the oil blob.

RAISING RAISINS

Put a few raisins into a bottle of clear soda and watch them rise and shimmy like they've come to life!

You'll need:

- A bottle of clear soda
- Raisins

The irregular surfaces of raisins hold some carbon dioxide from the carbonation in the soda, and when enough bubbles accumulate, they lift raisins to the surface.

WATER MIX-UP

You'll need:

- 2 identical jars
- Hot water, cold water
- Red and blue food coloring
- Index card or playing card

Fill one jar with hot tap water and add a drop of red food coloring. Fill a second jar with cold water and add a drop of blue food coloring. Slowly add more hot water to the red jar, until the water seems to flow over the top. Lay an index card on top of the red jar and tap gently. In a swift motion, turn the jar over. The card will prevent the water from spilling out. Now, place this upside-down red jar on top of the blue jar. Have a friend hold both jars steady as you pull the card out. A thin purple line will form where the colors meet, but the red and blue water will not mix.

Hot water is less dense than cold water. So, the cold water stays in the bottom jar, while the less dense hot water floats above it. What will happen if you put the cold blue water on top?

Experiments & Stunts

WATER SWING

Everyone knows that if you tip a bucket of water upside down you'll have a mess! Prove your friends wrong with this simple invention.

You'll need:

- Empty, clean yogurt or margarine container
- Hole punch
- Yarn, cord, or rope
- Water

Use a hole-punch and make three holes near the top of a plastic yogurt or margarine container. Thread three equal lengths of rope or heavy cord through the holes. Take the container outside and fill it halfway with water. Holding the cord, start swinging the water-filled container back and forth. Gradually make greater and greater arcs; eventually swing it in complete circles. Try swinging it horizontally over your head—like a cowboy's lasso. Did any of the water spill out? What happens if you swing the container slower and slower?

GLASS OF AIR

Wedge a paper napkin tightly in the bottom of a clear plastic glass or cup. Turn the glass over so its rim is down and sink it straight into a sink filled with water. Done right, the trapped air will prevent the water from entering the glass, and the napkin will stay high and dry. Pull the glass straight up out of the water and see what happens!

SECRET MESSAGE

You'll need:

- Lemon juice
- Pen cap
- Index card or thick paper
- A working light bulb

Dip a pen cap or some other pointy item into lemon juice and write your friend a message on an index card, postcard, or thick paper. When the juice dries, your writing will disappear! To read the message, hold the card up to a bare light bulb. The paper absorbs the lemon juice and natural light has a hard time reflecting such a pale color as yellow. When you hold the card up to a light bulb, you shed light on the lemon "ink."

45

QUICK CHANGE ARTIST

Demonstrate your power over the natural elements, changing colors at your command!

You'll need
- 1/4 cup grape juice
- Small, clear glass
- 1 tablespoon of baking soda
- 1 tablespoon of white vinegar

Pour the grape juice into the glass. Slowly mix the baking soda into the grape juice. The color at the top of the juice will change to blue. Now add the vinegar to the mixture, a drop at a time; the color will change to pink where the vinegar drips. Pour out the liquid in the sink and notice how dark it becomes.

Grape juice looks purple because its molecules are arranged in such a way that it absorbs all the colors of light except purple. Adding other substances changes the molecular structure of grape juice, so its color changes.

 LIGHTNING SPARKS

You'll need:
- Modeling clay
- Large metal paper clips
- Inflated balloon
- Wool sweater

Make a sculpture out of modeling clay, inserting several large metal paper clips somewhere into the design. Take the sculpture into a dark room or closet, and rub an inflated balloon against a wool sweater for 30 seconds. Hold the balloon close to, —but not touching—the paper clip. Sparks should jump between the balloon and the paper clips. Try rubbing the balloon against your hair, too.

TRULY TASTELESS EXPERIMENT

Convince your friends that they won't be able to taste the difference between an apple, an onion, and a potato. Place a blindfold around a friend's eyes. Make your friend hold her nose, then place a small piece of apple, potato, or onion on the center of her tongue. Ask your friend to identify the piece just by taste and without chewing. Do the same thing with the other two pieces of food.

Taste buds are tiny organs on your tongue that identify four basic tastes: salt, sweet, sour, and bitter. Since the center of your tongue has fewer taste buds than any other part of the tongue, it's hard to recognize foods that are only placed there.

WHAT SMELLS?

Have fun experimenting with smells! Collect several items that have distinctive smells: lemon, orange peel, perfume-soaked cotton, banana, pine needles, chocolate, coffee, dirt, vanilla, garlic, onion, mint, vinegar, moth balls, rose petals, saw dust, and pencil shavings. If you're brave enough, add some disgusting smells, too.

Keep the items separated and enclosed in plastic containers so that the odors do not mix. Blindfold a friend—or punch holes in the top of the containers to eliminate the need of a blindfold. Can your friends identify each item by smell? Do your friends have an immediate reaction to certain smells? Can they share memories associated with the smell?

VAMPIRE SOAP

You'll need:
- A small jar
- Laxative tablets
  (available from a grocery or drug store)
- Rubbing alcohol
- Soap and water

In a small jar, crush one or two laxative tablets and add a tablespoon of rubbing alcohol. Rub some of the mixture on your hand and allow it to dry. Then wash it off with soap. The soapy water turns bright red! Do not eat or drink the substance.

The laxative contains a substance called phenolphthalein, which turns bright red when it mixes with an alkali or a base like soap. By adding water you free some of the alkali, which then mixes with the phenolphthalein on your hand.

47

THAT'S HOT!

Create an exothermic chemical reaction! That sounds impressive! What it means is that you can create heat.

You'll need:
- Thermometer
- Bowl
- 1 Tablespoon of quick-rising dry yeast available from a grocery store
- 1/4 cup hydrogen peroxide
- Spoon

Look at the thermometer and see what temperature it is showing. Then put it in the bowl. Pour the hydrogen peroxide in the bowl, add the yeast, and stir with the spoon. Watch what happens! Feel the lower sides and bottom of the bowl. Wait a minute or two, then lift out the thermometer—what temperature is it showing?

When the yeast is mixed with the hydrogen peroxide, the molecules of the hydrogen peroxide change into oxygen and water. That change produces heat.

THAT'S COOL!

After impressing your friends by creating heat (see above), wow them by creating cold—an endothermic reaction.

You'll need:
- Thermometer
- 1 tablespoon of Epsom salts available from a grocery or drug store
- Lukewarm tap water
- Spoon
- One medium-sized jar

Fill the jar with tap water. Place the thermometer in the water and feel the temperature of the jar with your hands. After a few minutes, take out the thermometer, read what temperature it is recording, and put it back in the jar. Next, stir in the Epsom salts with the spoon and feel the jar again. Notice any difference? After a couple of minutes, take out the thermometer and check the temperature. Any change?

In a chemical change, sometimes heat is used up instead of created, and that's endothermic. The Epsom salts, which are magnesium sulfate, used the water's heat energy to split apart the ions of sulfate and magnesium, cooling the water.

EGG FLOAT

Make an egg float and astonish your friends! It's easy to do!

You'll need:
- Two large glasses
- Lukewarm water
- 1/2 cup salt
- Egg

Fill two large glasses with lukewarm water. Thoroughly dissolve about 1/2 cup of salt in one glass of water. Gather your audience around. Drop the egg into the unsalted water. It will sink to the bottom. Remove the egg and look sad, pretending your experiment never works. Now put the egg into the salt water, and your audience will be amazed to see the egg float.

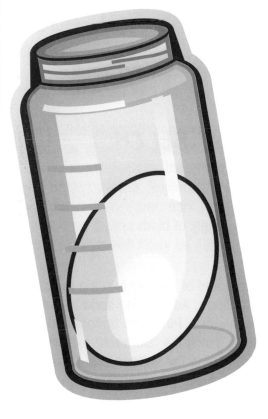

ADULT RUBBER EGGS

Make a quivering, rubbery egg sac!

You'll need:
- An egg
- Glass jar
- Vinegar

Place an egg in a jar. Pour in some vinegar until the egg is covered. Tiny bubbles will soon appear all over the shell. Over the next few hours the hard shell of the egg will disappear. The egg sac that surrounds the egg white and yolk, keeping them intact, will remain. Handle this "rubber" egg carefully, or you'll have a big mess on your hands! The vinegar is an acid that dissolves the calcium in the shell.

ADULT EGG IN A BOTTLE

How do you get a shelled, hard-boiled egg into a narrow-necked bottle without damaging the egg? Easy!

You'll need:
- Cooking oil, butter, or margarine
- An eight-ounce glass baby bottle
- Two small, shelled, hard-boiled eggs
- A piece of paper, four inches square
- Matches
- Adult supervision

Rub the oil, butter, or margarine around the inside of the mouth of the bottle. Fold the paper to form an accordion. Carefully light one end of the paper with a match, and drop it into the bottle. Quickly place the egg onto the mouth of the bottle. You did it!

BARKING SEALS!

With a little practice, you'll be able to get this simple looking experiment to sound like barking seals have invaded your house.

You'll need:
- Several paper cups—a variety of sizes, styles
- Several toothpicks
- Water
- Yarn
- Scissors
- Pencil

Cut off several pieces of yarn, each one a different length. Soak the yarn pieces in water for several minutes. While the yarn is soaking, take a paper cup and poke a small hole right in the middle of the bottom using a sharp pencil. Take a piece of the wet yarn and carefully push one end through the hole in the bottom of the cup. Tightly tie the end in the cup around the middle of a toothpick. Drop the toothpick into the cup so that it lies flat on the bottom of the cup—you may have to break off some of the toothpick until it fits. Wet your fingers, tightly pinch the yarn between your thumb and forefinger just below the cup, and pull down—hard. If you have trouble making a sound, add more water to the yarn and/or your fingers. Experiment with different lengths of yarn. Try a different kind of cup—maybe use a foam cup or a tiny paper bathroom cup.
Notice any differences?

Pulling your fingers down the length of the yarn causes the yarn to vibrate. The vibrations travel up the yarn and into the cup; the cup and the air inside the cup vibrate, too.

Gross & Not-So-Gross

Games

GROSS EATING CONTEST

Ahead of time, fill two paper grocery bags with food items that smell or feel gross—nothing spoiled! Each bag must have the same items. Suggestions: raw onions, cold beans, cooked spaghetti, hardboiled eggs, black olives, cheese chunks, and lunchmeat. Divide your friends or family members into two teams. The first player on each team takes one item from the bag, eats it completely, and then passes the bag to the next player. The first team to eat all the food items in the bag is the winner!

BELCHING CONTEST

Players try burping as many letters in the alphabet as they can. Whoever makes it the furthest through the alphabet wins! Give prizes for the loudest burps, softest burps, most disgusting burps… ooooo, yuck!

SODA ROULETTE

You'll need a can of soda for each player. Vigorously shake one can of soda. Mix the cans up. Each player chooses a can, puts it up to his nose, and on the count of three opens it! Who is the unlucky winner?

MIND READER

One of your friends must think of a person, place, or thing! You must read her mind! You can only ask questions that she can answer by saying "yes" or "no." How many questions will you have to ask? Now, it's your turn to think of a person, place, or thing and your friend's turn to ask questions.

53

ALPHABETICAL TALL TALE

Choose a subject—any subject! Maybe the subject is scary movies, or disgusting foods, or an alien invasion from outer space, or a mad scientist and an experiment that's gone wrong—any subject that will make a great story. Now, begin the story. The first player says a sentence beginning with the letter "A." The second player adds more to the story, beginning a sentence with the letter "B." Try to get as far down the alphabet as you can. It's harder than it sounds!

Example: *"Aliens have invaded!"*
"Bravo! "
"Cool kids are trying to capture the aliens."
"Demented doctors are attempting to destroy the aliens!"
"French Fries! That's what aliens prefer to eat, French fries!"

For more challenging fun, try to tell the story asking only questions! Every player must ask a question that begins with the letter of the alphabet.

 ## CANDY THROW UP

Most of your friends know what it feels like to have eaten too much candy! But do they know what their favorite candies look like when they've …let's say, come back up? Ahead of time, ask an adult to help you melt 6-10 candy bars in individual cupcake or muffin liners in microwave. (Be certain to write down what candy bar you melted in each container!) Players pass and smell each container of candy throw-up and write down what name brand candy product they believe was "regurgitated."

For even more disgusting fun, put the melted candies in disposable diapers. Your friends must smell each diaper and guess what candy the baby passed!

PIG

You and a small group of friends will quickly pass the time with this classic game of strategy and chance.

You'll need:
- A die
- Paper
- Pencil

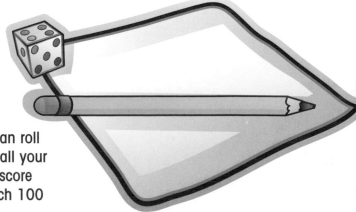

Take turns rolling a die and adding up your points. You can roll as many times as you want, but if you roll a 1, you lose all your points for that turn. When you choose to stop, write your score and pass the die to the next player. The first player to reach 100 points wins.

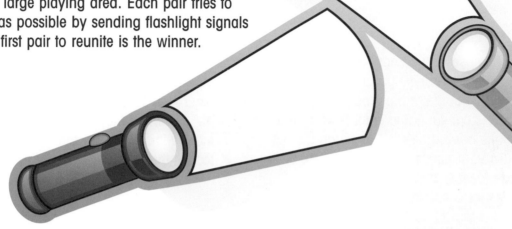

FLASHLIGHT SIGNALS

Play this game outside after dark with a large group of friends. Every player will need a flashlight! To begin, pair off with another friend, and create your own unique flashlight signal—for example, one short and one long flash followed by three short flashes. The partners separate and go to opposite ends of a large playing area. Each pair tries to reunite as quickly as possible by sending flashlight signals to each other. The first pair to reunite is the winner.

POP UP MINUTE

Okay, just how long do you think a minute really is? What about two minutes, five minutes? Try this with a group of friends. Out of sight of any clocks or watches, ask your friends to stand up when they feel one minute is up! You, holding a watch say, "Go." The friend who stands up closest to the minute is the winner. For more fun, try two minutes, three minutes, or even five minutes.

BEAT THE BUNNY

The object of the game is for the farmer to catch the bunny. No, we're not talking about a real farmer trapping a real bunny! This is a really fast game to play with a group of friends. You'll need two balls of different sizes. Players sit on the floor in a circle. Begin passing the bunny—the small ball—from player to player around the circle. When the bunny is about half way around, start passing the farmer—the large ball—in the same direction. Can players pass the farmer fast enough to catch up with the bunny? For more challenging play, the farmer can change directions, but the bunny can only go one way.

GROSS SONGS
and annoying
kids love to sing!

ODDS/EVENS

Play this game with another friend when you have a few minutes to spare. (This is great fun while waiting for your food at a sit-down restaurant—just don't get too loud!) One of you chooses to be "odds" and the other chooses to be "evens." Both of you make a fist, shake it, say, "One, two, three...shoot," and stick out one or two fingers. Count the fingers that are sticking out. If the total is an odd number, the player who picked odds wins that number of points; and the same goes for evens. The first player to reach 50 points wins.

GHOST

Next time you have several friends together, try this challenging spelling and bluffing game. To start, one friend says a letter of the alphabet. Each friend adds a letter but is careful not to spell a word. If a player does make a word he's the ghost and is out of the game. On your turn, try to say a letter that forces the next player to make a word. But be careful, because the next player may challenge you and ask what word you're spelling! If you can't give a word you lose the challenge and are out of the game. But if you do have a word in mind, the challenger loses and is out of the game. For even more fun, players who complete a word or lose a challenge must do a stunt acceptable to the group.

FAST TALKER

Now you can prove who in your group of friends talks too much! Challenge each friend to talk non-stop for one minute about a subject you choose. It's harder than you think! If the player hesitates or stops talking he is out of the game. You'll need someone with a watch or stopwatch to time each player. For more challenging play, have two friends talk at the same time about that topic for one minute.

WHERE'S "IT"?

Play this twisted game of Hide and Seek outside after dark! "It" hides while all the other kids count to 50. Everyone looks for "It," but when they find him each quietly hides with "It." Soon, those who are left realize that they alone are looking for "It."

BLANKET STAND

Spread out a blanket on the floor. The object of the game is to have your entire group of friends on the blanket so that no arms, legs, or other body parts are touching the ground off the blanket. If this is too easy, have your friends get off the blanket, fold the blanket in half, and try again. Keep folding the blanket in half! Soon, you'll end up in a big pile! Guaranteed!

WORMS IN A PIE

You'll need gummy worms, whipped cream, and aluminum pie plates or deep disposable plates—one for each person playing the game. Place the same amount of gummy worms on each plate and cover them with whipped cream. Blind fold each player. On the count of three, each player dips into the pie with their mouth, trying to pull out as many worms as they can. See who can pull out the most worms in a time limit or just set a certain amount of worms to find. For more fun, and if everyone is willing, put all the gummy worms and whipped cream in one large container and let players search together.

PUTT, PUTT GOLF

Miniature golfing every day may be out of the question! But here is a fun, inexpensive way to practice your game at home or at a restaurant while you wait for your food to arrive!

You'll need:
- Plain paper
- Markers, crayons
- Blindfolds—if you don't trust players to close their eyes!

Use a large sheet of copy paper or construction paper. Draw the fairway—an odd, oblong shape. At one end draw a line for the tee (or starting point). At the far end of the fairway draw a small circle—this is the hole! Now, place a marker, crayon, or pencil down at the tee, close your eyes, and try to draw a line to the hole! Open your eyes and lift the marker; that's your shot. Add a stroke if you strayed outside the boundaries. The next player then tees off on the same sheet. Play again, beginning where your last stroke ended. Your score is the number of shots it takes you to reach the hole. Play nine holes or even 18 like the pros.

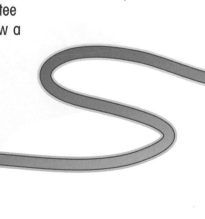

"STICKY FINGERS"

Choose one friend to be "Sticky Fingers." In this game of tag, when "Sticky Fingers" tags you, place your hand on the place he touched and continue to run. As more and more friends become stuck on themselves, "Sticky Fingers" has a better chance to totally immobilize someone. A third touch and you're out of the game.

SNAKE IN THE GRASS

Mark off a small playing area outside. One friend is the snake, and lies on the ground on his stomach. Everyone gathers fearlessly around him. When you shout, "Snake in the grass" everyone moves, staying within the playing area. The snake, moving on his belly, tries to tag as many as he can. If you're tagged, you become a snake, too. The last person caught is the snake starter in the next game. Make the playing area fairly small.

ANKLE WRESTLING

First, mark off a small playing area. Next, choose two friends to enter the ring, stoop over, and grasp their ankles. The object of the game is to push your opponent over or to make him let go of his ankles. The player is automatically disqualified if he steps out of the ring. Set up a tournament with friends and family and declare an Ankle Wrestling Champ.

SOCK WRESTLING

Mark off a small play area. Players take off their shoes, but leave on their socks and move around the ring. The idea of the game is for players to somehow remove a sock from their opponents. It can be played one-on-one or with several players in the ring at the same time. Players who lose both socks must leave the ring.

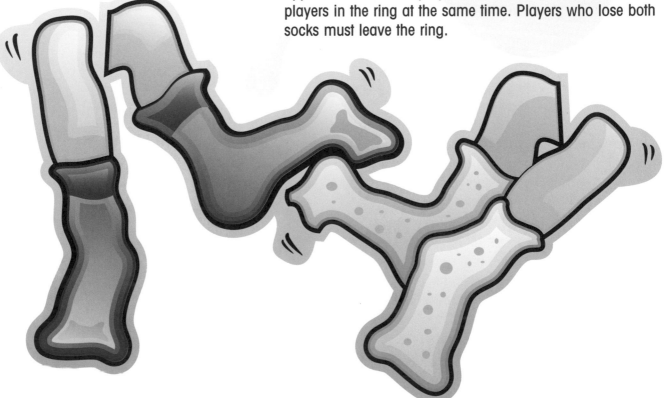

TEENY-TINY SCAVENGER HUNT

Send your friends outside in search of as many different natural items as they can find that fit in a small, plastic condiment container. Consider awarding points for each unique item collected, and extra points for live creatures that will be returned to nature, of course! If you go to a park be certain you have permission to disturb or remove natural items from the grounds.

NAUSEATING NATURE HUNT

If the Teeny-Tiny Scavenger Hunt is too tame for your tastes, search instead for icky, nasty natural items.

Make a list of icky items and the points that will be earned for each item that is found. Take a grocery bag and go out into the yard to find the items. Whoever gets the most points, wins.

Icky Items May Include:
- A dead moth
- Spoonful of tree sap
- Daddy long-legs
- Green caterpillar guts
- Squished berries
- A four-leaf clover
- A live slug
- A live worm
- Ants
- Moss
- Stinkweed
- A dead fly
- Snake
- Cricket

SPUD

Gather your friends together, everyone touching home base, and have each player count off. One player who is "It" throws a ball high in the air and calls out one player's number. As the other players scatter, the called player catches the ball and shouts, "Spud!" The other players must immediately freeze. The ball holder takes two giant steps toward any player, and tries to hit that player with the ball. The target person can try to dodge the ball by moving his body but not his feet. If the thrower misses OR the target catches the ball, the thrower earns an S. If he hits the target, that person earns an S. Whoever earns the letter becomes the next "It" and begins the next round. Players are eliminated once they earn S-P-U-D.

KNOTS

Stand your friends in a circle facing each other, shake hands with the person directly across from you, and join left hands with a different person in the group. Now, try to untangle the human knot without letting go of your hands. Try doing this with different size groups.

MAGIC NUMBER

The object of the game is to force a player to say the Magic Number. To play, first choose a magic number—almost any number that you can count to quickly! On your turn, say only one OR two numbers next in the sequence. For example, say the magic number is 20. Player one counts "One, Two." The next player may say, "Three, Four." The next player may say, "Five." Play continues until a player is forced to say 20, the Magic Number. That player is out of the game. Continue playing until a champion is named! This game requires concentration and forward thinking!

FORTUNATELY-UNFORTUNATELY

Look at the bright side of things in a silly way! For example, you say, "Unfortunately, there's a big brown bear in the car." Your friend says, "Fortunately, he doesn't eat girls." Another friend says, "Unfortunately, he's looking at me and licking his lips." You say, "Fortunately, I brought along my brown-bear-catching sword." Continue alternating between fortunate and unfortunate things until everyone breaks down with laughter.

Games

GRASS BLADE SYMPHONY

With a blade of grass and a little practice, anyone can make beautiful music! Try this stunt with several friends and soon your unusual musical talents will annoy everyone nearby.

First, find a nice wide blade of grass, about as long as your first finger. Make a loose fist, with your thumb pointing upwards and your thumbnail towards you. Now, lick the edge of your thumb from wrist to tip and stick the blade where you licked. Sure, it's gross, but the moisture keeps the blade of grass from falling off. Then bring your other hand and thumb up so that the grass is trapped between your thumbs. You should see a gap between the first and second joints of your thumb where the grass is not touching either thumb. Be sure that the grass is stretched tightly in this gap. Put your thumbs to your mouth, so that this gap is against your lips. Pucker your lips, as if you were going to blow out a candle, and blow hard. If you do it just right, you will hear a loud sound. Depending on the shape of the blade of grass, how tight it is, and how hard you blow, you may get anything from a low rasp to a loud, shrill whistle. With some practice, you can make a variety of sounds.

TOOTHPASTE AND GERMS

Divide your friends into two teams, "Toothpaste" and "Germs" respectively. Send team Toothpaste to one side of the playground or yard and team Germs to the other side. The leader gives each side commands in turn. For example, "Germs, advance 3," and then the Germs take 3 steps forward. "Toothpaste, retreat 2," and the Toothpaste go 2 steps backwards. Once you have them reasonably near to each other say, "Toothpaste (or Germs) ATTACK." Then the team you have chosen chases the others back to their safety. Any players tagged then join the other side and the game starts again. Keep it going for as long as you need!

CLOUD WATCHING

If you can't go out after dark and count the stars, head to a hillside or wide-open space, stretch out on a blanket and look up at clouds in the sky! What shapes are they making? Time them to see how fast they float by.

STAR GAZING

Spend an hour or two after dark, kicking back on a hillside, looking up at the night sky. Have several binoculars to share—perhaps a telescope —and count the stars, play imaginary dot to dot with the stars or make up stories about the stars. For more serious learning, use constellation guide maps and try to locate the constellations.

GROSS SONGS
and annoying
kids love to sing!

SPITBALL TARGET PRACTICE

You'll never want to play darts again after using spit-wads instead! First, make a target on a piece of poster board, like a dartboard with circles and points marked off. (Of course, with permission, you might draw your dartboard on a sliding glass door using dry-erase or washable markers.) Next, each player must make his arsenal of spitballs. Give each player a different color piece of paper. Each player shreds the paper into small pieces, wets them in his mouth, rolling them into tiny balls with his tongue. Finally, give each player a straw. Aiming ONLY at the target, load one spitball (or two, or three!) and blow them out! Keep score, adding up the points of each spitball that actually sticks! Never blow the spit wads at someone else!

100

50

30

thhht!

thhht!

thhht!

BOBBING FOR APPLES

This classic game is perfect on a hot day! Put several apples in a large tub or wading pool. Players try to grab one using only their mouth. For more fun, add ice cubes to the water.

Try this with younger kids: Cut several apple shapes out of construction paper and place a loop of masking tape on each one. Place the apples in a large clothesbasket, box, or pan. To bob for the apples, a blindfolded player must get an apple by touching his nose to the masking tape!

FACE-TO-FACE

Choose one player to stand in the center, while the rest of you stand in a large circle face-to-face with a partner. The player in the middle calls out commands such as "Face-to-face," "Back-to-back," "Side-to-side," or "Knee-to-Knee." Players take these positions accordingly. When the person in the middle calls "All change!" all the players must find a new partner! The person in the middle tries to find a partner, too. The person left without a partner becomes the new person in the middle and starts to give commands.

Games

ICE FISHING

Ahead of time fill several large buckets with ice water and marbles. Hide the buckets until time to play. Divide your friends into teams. Everyone removes their shoes and socks. Explain that in this relay race, each team member runs to the bucket, puts his bare foot into the water, pulls out as many marbles as possible on just one try using only toes, places the marbles in a container, and runs back to the team. The next player repeats. Of course, leave out the detail about ice water! The team that pulls the most marbles from the ice water is the winner.

MASTER AND COMMANDER

Have your friends sit in a circle on the floor. Choose one person to leave the room for a few minutes. While that friend is out of the room, choose one person in the group to be the Master and Commander. Everyone in the group repeats the actions of the Master and Commander. If he scratches his nose, everyone slowly begins to scratch their noses, too. If the Master and Commander places his hands behind his head, everyone else slowly places their hands behind their heads. After you've practiced following the Master and Commander, bring the first person back into the room. The object of the game is for that person to guess who is the Master and Commander. When the Master and Commander is revealed, he leaves the room and becomes the next person to guess.

WATER BALLOON VOLLEYBALL

Form several teams. Team members each hold on to the sides of an old bed sheet or large beach towel. Work together to toss a water balloon to the other team. Keep score, if you want, as you would in regular volleyball matches.

ICE MELT

Ahead of time, fill several half-gallon milk containers with water and freeze. Add a toy action figure to each container. To play, give each team one block of ice with the carton removed. The first team to rescue the action figure by melting their block of ice using only their hands is the winner. Consider allowing team members to use their feet and other body parts, too—but this can be, well, a little gross! Another option is to melt the ice by pouring warm water over the ice block.

WINK

One friend leaves the room. The remaining players sit in a circle and select their group leader. The first friend returns to the center of the circle. Now, the group leader secretly winks at another player seated around the circle; that player waits several seconds and then falls or collapses, pretending to gag, fall to the floor in pain, or just faint. The leader continues to secretly wink at other players who each collapse. The object is for the friend in the center to identify the secret leader. At any time the player may point to someone in the circle and say, "I accuse you." When the secret leader is revealed, he leaves the room and becomes the next person to guess.

WATER TIME BOMB

Poke a hole in a balloon before filling it with water. Now the water balloon is a time bomb with a slow leak. Players stand in a circle and toss the balloon around. The object is not to be the one holding the balloon when it runs out of water.

WRAPPER LAUNCH

Wrap a foil gum wrapper around your thumb. Leave about a third hanging off. Make a cap on the end by twisting the top of the wrapper on your thumb. Now, take the wrapper off your thumb. Make a fist with a hollow tube inside. Gently push the wrapper cap, hollow-side down, deep into the circle formed by your thumb and index finger. With the flattened palm of your free hand strike the base of your fist with the gum wrapper. The wrapper cap should launch into the air because of the air pressure forced on it by your fist. Get your friends together, enjoy some gum, and have a contest to see who can pop the highest rocket.

NOSE GUM

On a large piece of poster board draw a bull's-eye target. Tape the poster board to a clean wall. Give each player a piece of gum to chew for a few minutes. Blindfold one player at a time and spin them around. Instruct the player to take the gum out of his mouth, stick it to his nose, and then try to stick the gum to the target. Whoever gets the closest to the bull's-eye is the winner.

GUM SCULPTURES

Give each of your friends two or three pieces of bubble gum, an index card, and a toothpick. Let them chew the gum for several minutes. Each player then designs a sculpture with the bubble gum using the toothpick as a tool.

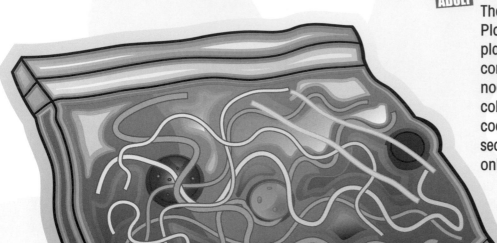

LOST EYEBALLS

ADULT

The lost eyeballs are really marbles! Place the marbles in a medium-size plastic storage container. Fill the container with cooked spaghetti noodles doctored up with a red food coloring and a small amount of cooking oil. Players take turns searching for the lost eyeballs using only their bare feet.

SQUISH PAINTING

ADULT

Put a small amount of ketchup and/or mustard inside a large zip-lock sandwich or storage bag. Squeeze out the air and tightly seal the bag. Lay the bag flat, and spread the contents evenly. Draw on the bag with your fingers. Smooth over the bag to erase the drawing. What other mixtures can you place in the bag? Try pudding!

TOE PAINTING

ADULT

Instead of finger painting, try toe painting! With adult help and supervision, hang a large piece of paper, white paper tablecloth or even a bed sheet on a wall. Be sure to use a drop cloth, too, if you do this inside the house. Kids dip their toes into pie pans or small plastic containers of different color paints. Watercolors or acrylic paints will work well. Divide your friends into teams and award prizes for the most creative, funniest, and scariest paintings. Have a container of warm soapy water and towels nearby to wash and dry each artist's toes!

POOR KITTY

No one will be able to keep a straight face for very long with this silly game. Everyone sits on the floor in a circle. Choose one friend to be the Poor, Poor Kitty. The Poor, Poor Kitty goes up to another friend in the circle purring and meowing, acting like a cat. The friend must pat the kitty on the head and say, "Poor, Poor Kitty" without laughing. If the player laughs, then he must become the kitty and try to make others around the circle laugh.

SUN CATCHERS

Collect soft, colorless plastic lids from coffee cans and margarine tubs. Draw the outline of a creature or geometric shape with a black permanent marker. Carefully cut out the shape with scissors. Completely fill in the shape with colored permanent markers. When the design is finished, punch a hole in the top of the shape and tie a loop of string or thread. Hang your sun catcher from the top of a window or string a few together to make a mobile.

SNOW SCULPTURES

Mix up some wintertime fun no matter what time of year it is or where you live! In a large bowl mix 2 cups of mild, powdered laundry detergent, add water, and whip with an electric mixer until doughy. Mold and sculpt the snow mixture. When you're finished, allow the sculpture to dry. The snow will dry bright white.

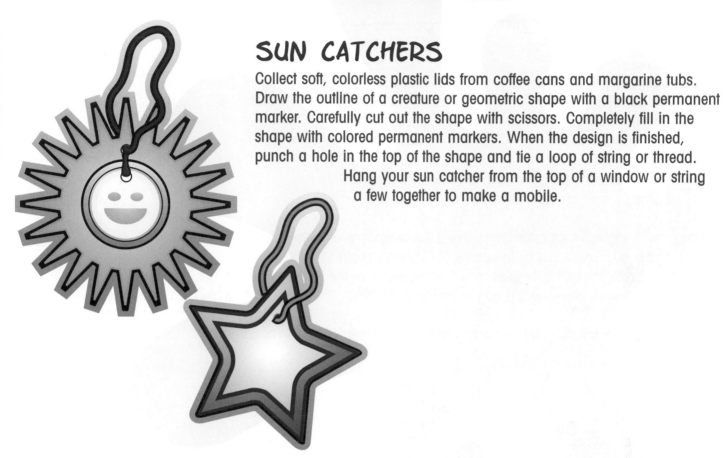

GROSS SONGS
and annoying
kids love to sing!

BLUE GOOP

All kids love goop—called by any number of gross and disgusting names! Follow this recipe to make your own goop.

You'll need:

- White glue
- Water
- 2 paper cups
- Blue food coloring
- Borax laundry detergent available from a grocery store
- Small plastic storage container

Mix together 2 tablespoons of white glue and 2 tablespoons of water in a paper cup. In another paper cup, mix together ten drops of blue food coloring, 1/4 cup of water, and 3/4 teaspoon of borax laundry detergent. Add 2 tablespoons of the borax mixture to the glue mixture and stir well. Have fun playing with your Blue Goop. Store it in an airtight container.

To avoid stains, be careful not to let Blue Goop touch furniture, carpet, or clothing.

RUBBERBAND BALL

To make your own bouncy ball, pinch together the ends of a single rubber band and tie it into a loose double knot. Wrap and twist a second band around the knot repeatedly, until it is taut. Continue adding rubber bands one at a time until the ball is as large as you like, or you run out of bands. You also can speed along the process by covering an inner core of wadded-up newspaper or aluminum foil with rubber bands.

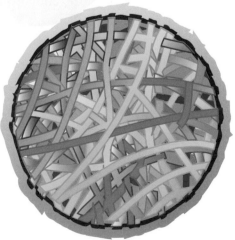

OUR TOWN

Name yourself as the mayor of this homemade city!

You'll need:
- Brown or white paper lunch bags
- Newspapers
- Markers, crayons, paint
- Construction paper, fabric scraps and other art materials

Build an entire city of brown paper lunch bags. Use two bags for each building. On one bag draw or color a building—either horizontally or vertically. Add bricks or siding, sketch in doors and windows, window boxes, stairwells, signs, and even people! Next, stuff the second bag with crumpled newspaper and slip the decorated bag on top. Cut out signs, awnings, chimneys, overhanging rooftops, and doors from colored paper, and glue them onto the buildings. Set up the city on the floor or on a table.

ALIEN INVASION

Okay, so they haven't really come from outer space to take over the world. These one-of-a-kind aliens are still fun to make!

You'll need:
- Balloons
- Cardboard, poster board
- Markers
- Scissors

To make each alien, first make its feet or base: cut out a heart or butterfly shape from poster board or cardboard. Draw on shoes or toes with markers, crayons, or paint. When done, cut a 1/2-inch slit between the heels. Blow up a balloon for each pair of feet and knot the end. Using markers, carefully draw the alien's face and body directly on the balloon. Slip the knotted end of the balloon into the slit between the feet. Stand your alien balloons around the room, or place them where unsuspecting friends will find them.

69

GUMDROP CONSTRUCTION PROJECT

Empty a bag of gumdrops, set out a package of toothpicks, and start to build! Begin making and combining triangles and squares. Experiment and discover what formations are sturdier and stronger. The candies will dry out and crumble—so don't plan on saving the creations! Here's another great idea—demolish the project with a Gumdrop Eating Contest!

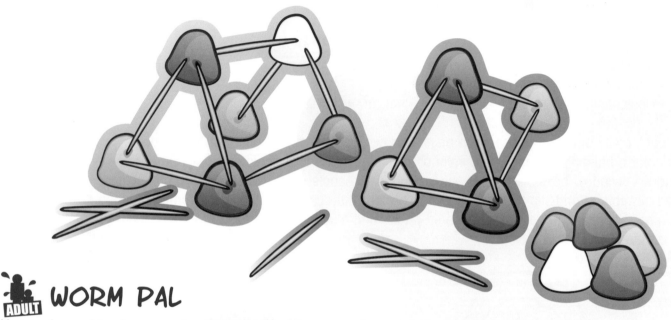

⬛ADULT WORM PAL

You and your friends can make and care for your own pet worms! For more fun, make an extra long snake!

You'll need:
- Fabric scraps
- Sewing machine or needle and thread
- Stuffing material—available at a craft or discount store
- Craft wire or thin wire coat hanger cut as long as your worm
- Pins
- Scissors

Measure and cut a 3-inch by 12-inch rectangle from scrap fabric—fleece material works well. Fold the fabric in half lengthwise, right side together (inside out), and pin. Carefully round the corners with the scissors—after all no one has ever seen a square-ended worm! Now, carefully sew along the edges, leaving one end open. Turn the worm right side out. Insert craft wire or even a wire coat hanger cut to the length of your worm. Fill the worm with stuffing, keeping the wire in the center. When the worm is stuffed full, sew the end together. Bend and shape your new pet worm. Add eyes, a tongue, stripes, dots, and other markings with paint or glued-on fabric scraps.

ADULT GRUESOME MONSTER HEADS

These shrunken apple heads may take some time, but they're guaranteed to be a scream!

You'll need:
- Peeled apples
- Small paring knife
- Supplies for making hair and facial features—yarn, beads, feathers, dried beans, rice, pasta, toothpicks, and beads
- Craft sticks
- Cups or mugs

With adult supervision, carefully carve eyes, nose, and a mouth into each peeled apple. Don't worry if the carvings aren't perfect—this will make the head look even creepier. Poke rice, beans, dried corn, raisins, or pasta into the apple to make facial features and hair. Be creative! When finished, push a craft stick into the bottom of each apple, and prop upright in a cup or mug in a warm, dry place. Make sure the apple is not touching the side of the cup. Visit the monsters-in-progress every few days. When the apple heads begin to turn leathery you can change facial expressions by gently twisting, pushing, pulling, turning, and rearranging items. In a few weeks you'll have really gruesome monster heads.

CRACKER CASTLE

Forget the gingerbread cookies! Build a fairytale castle with assorted crackers and peanut butter instead!

You'll need:
- Assorted crackers
- Peanut butter
- Raisins, nuts, candy pieces, etc.
- Cookie sheet or wax paper

Build your castle on a cookie sheet or large piece of waxed paper. Use plain soda crackers, large and bite-sized butter crackers, club crackers, square wheat crackers, graham crackers, round vanilla wafers, and sandwich cookies. Set crackers vertically, gluing them to each other with peanut butter. You might want to spread a peanut butter foundation and set the crackers into it. Glue smaller crackers onto larger ones to make doors, window shutters, columns, and stairs. Use plain or cinnamon graham crackers for sloped roofs. Add raisins, cereal, pasta, seeds, or anything else that can be attached with peanut butter.

SPIDER WEB T-SHIRTS

You'll need:

- An old white t-shirt
- Black dye
- An old bucket
- Rubber bands
- Permanent markers or fabric paint

What to do:

1. Fill a bucket with black dye following the package directions.
2. Lay an old white t-shirt flat on the table. Pull the t-shirt up from the center and put rubber bands around the "wad" of material. Continue pulling up from the center and adding more rubber bands. The more rubber bands you use, the more your shirt will look like a spider's web.
3. Submerge the whole t-shirt in the bucket of black dye. Follow the package directions. The longer you leave the shirt in the dye, the darker your spider's web will become.
4. Remove the t-shirt from the dye, carefully wring out the excess water, and lay the shirt flat on the floor or table. Allow the shirt to dry completely before removing the rubber bands.
5. Use a permanent marker or fabric paint to draw your spider in its web.

FOIL MASK

You'll need:

- Heavy-duty aluminum foil
- Scissors
- Permanent markers

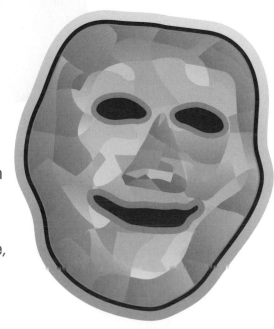

Cut a 24-by-12-inch piece of heavy-duty aluminum foil. Fold the foil into a 12-inch square. Working together with a friend, press the foil onto your friend's face, making sure to mold it over his cheekbones, nose, lips, and eye sockets. Carefully pull the mask away. Now, have your friend mold your face mask. Use scissors to cut eye, nose, and mouth holes. Add colorful details with a permanent marker, pressing down gently.

BALLOON ORCHESTRA

Everyone in the orchestra holds a balloon. Together, blow up the balloons in unison, pinch the neck closed and let out the air a squeak at a time to the rhythm of some easily recognized song like "Home On The Range" or "Jingle Bells." To end the skit every orchestra member may let go at the director's signal.

STRONG COFFEE

Set a large pan of dirty water in the center of the stage. You and three of your friends each walk one at a time to the pan, carrying a coffee mug, dip the mug in, bring it up to your lips for a drink, and say:

> **1st friend: "This coffee is getting worse!"**
>
> **2nd friend: "This tea is getting worse!"**
>
> **3rd friend: "This chocolate is getting worse!"**

The fourth friend, walks to pan, dips his hands in and takes out a pair of dirty, wet socks. As he wrings them out he says, "I thought that would get them clean!"

SUCKER'S BET

Dare your friends to drink water from a jar through a straw! They're sure to fail with this simple prank. You'll need:
- Glass jar with a metal lid
- Hammer and Nail
- Drinking straw
- Modeling clay
- Water

Make a hole big enough for the straw in the metal jar lid using a hammer and nail. Fill the jar about halfway with water and replace the lid. Insert a straw through the hole in the lid; then plug the hole up tight with clay around the straw, so that no air can get in. Now, challenge your friend to drink the water in the jar through the straw. Watch how frustrated your friend becomes when the water doesn't budge! By sealing the lid, you've blocked the air pressure and the water can't rise.

THE LAWNMOWER

(One friend is on his hands and knees pretending to be a lawnmower.)

Owner: *(Yanking imaginary rope, while mower sputters)* This old mower, I can't get it going. I need some help. *(Gets help from another friend.)*

Helper #1: So you just want me to yank on this rope, and get it started? That's easy! *(Yanking rope)*

Lawnmower: *(Sputters, bobs up and down)*

Helper #1: I'm sorry. I can't seem to do it. Have you checked the gas?

Owner: Yes, I have. Thanks anyway. Well, let's see who else has a strong arm. *(Selects another friend.)* What I need you to do is to give a real good yank on the starting rope and make it run.

Helper #2: Sure thing. *(Yanks rope a couple of times.)*

Lawnmower: *(Bobs up and down, sputters, coughs)*

Helper #2: Sorry, I can't do it either.

Owner: What I need is someone big and strong. *(Select another person and get him to pull the rope)*

Mower: *(Splutters, coughs, begins to vibrate and run)*

Owner: There. All it needed was a real jerk.

Pranks & Skits

THE IMPORTANT PAPERS

The setting can be either a king or a boss in his office who instructs an assistant to bring royal or important papers. Your friend runs in with a stack of papers. The king or boss is quite upset, tosses the papers aside, and demands that the assistant bring him his really important papers. Other people bring in other stacks of papers one at a time. The king throws them aside and becomes more and more upset, angrily insisting that he have his important papers. At last someone comes in with a roll of bathroom tissue. The king knights or the boss promotes the assistant, thanking him profusely before running off the stage in visible relief.

LET ONE RIP!

Place a book or dollar bill out in the open. Wait for someone to come over and pick it up. When the person bends over, rip a piece of cloth. How many people will reach back to see if their clothing ripped?

THE LITTLE GREEN BALL

The first friend enters and says, "Oh no I've lost it!" He then starts to search around on the floor. The second friend comes in and asks what the first person is looking for. The first person replies that he has lost his little green ball. Both continue searching the floor. Several more friends come on and are told about the lost little green ball. Even members of the audience can be persuaded to join in the search. The key is to be melodramatic, exaggerating movements and words. After enough time has been dragged out, the first person sticks a finger up his nose and says, "Don't worry! I can make another one!" YUK!!!!!

THE LEGEND OF HERBERT SMEAR...

ADULT

Tell ghost stories in the dark and pass around the bowls of the items below. Another option is to blindfold your friends, have them sit in a circle on the floor, and pass the body parts around the circle for each to feel as you tell the horrific tale.

Brains: An overcooked head of cauliflower

Eyes: Olives or peeled grapes

Live Worms: Gummy worms—not as scary though

Intestines: Soggy marshmallows, strung together

Zombie Hair: Dried corn silk from ears of corn

Barf/Vomit: Chunky salsa and canned corn mixed together

Teeth: Dried popcorn kernels

Decaying Flesh: Mashed potatoes topped with instant potato flakes, add coloring

Veins: Cooked spaghetti

Maggots: Cooked mini pasta shells, or rice

Breaking Bones: Fresh crisp celery or dog biscuits

Scrambled Brains: Lumpy cottage cheese

GLASS OF WATER

Place a glass of water in the middle of the stage. The first friend crawls across the floor crying for water, but dies dramatically shortly after beginning his crawl. The second friend dies just short of the glass of water. The third friend on his last bit of strength really hams up his thirst and desperation as much as possible. But reaching the water, he takes out a comb, grooms his hair with the water, sighs with relief, and goes off stage.

PUPPY IN THE BOX

Props: A cardboard box, and a stuffed dog or animal.

Announcer:	This scene takes place on the street outside a grocery store. *(Several friends are gathered, chatting outside the store.)*
Michael:	(Enters holding the box) Hi guys! Would you please hold this box for me while I go into the store? *(Exits)*
Nathan:	I wonder what's in the box?
Jason:	I don't know, but something yellow is leaking out!
Bob:	*(Rubs finger against the bottom of box then licks finger.)* Hmmm, it tastes like lemon soda.
Nathan:	*(Also rubs box and licks finger.)* No. I think it's more like chicken soup.
Michael:	*(Returns, looks into the box.)* Oh, you naughty puppy!

CANDY STORE

This is great in a large group of people, with unsuspecting friends and family chosen to participate. Announce that you are the proud new owner of a candy store! You need the help of your friends to build and furnish your store. Choose people to be the doors, shelves, cash registers, signs, and other items in the store. Each person has an action to do. For example, the "revolving door" may stand and rotate when you push on his outstretched arms. The "cash register" may stand with her arms out front and fingers up—like a drawer—and say, "Cha-Ching" whenever you touch her nose. "Signs" might stand with their arms spread wide, repeatedly flash their open palms, and grin from ear-to-ear. Quickly move back and forth between each item, keeping them all in motion! Be creative and try to involve as many good sports as possible. Ahead of time clue in one friend who asks, "If this is a candy store, where's all the candy?" You reply, "What are you talking about? Have you ever seen so many suckers?" while gesturing to all the friends on stage around you!

DANDRUFF FLAKES

Put small amounts of cornstarch or finely crushed instant oatmeal in your hair. Be sure to scratch it out for all your friends to see!

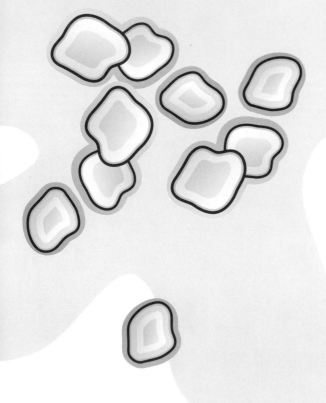

BROWNIE SURPRISE

Serve this chewy treat to your unsuspecting friends! Take a brand-new kitchen sponge and cover it with a thick coat of chocolate frosting. Add sprinkles and arrange on a plate.

Pranks & Skits

TAKE A SHOWER, PLEASE!

Put a rubber band around the handle of the kitchen sink sprayer when nobody's looking. This automatically keeps the nozzle in spray mode. Make sure the nozzle is pointing up and outward. The next person to use the sink will take a shower!

ALIEN MILK

Serve your favorite breakfast cereal, but add green food coloring to the milk container before it's poured. This works best with an opaque milk container—one you can't see through! The looks on your friends' faces should be priceless.

GOT CHANGE?

Superglue several coins to the sidewalk or any spot that has a lot of people walking nearby. Make sure it's an appropriate place, then watch people break fingernails to get the coins.

79

ARCTIC CEREAL

Tomorrow's breakfast will be unforgettable with this simple, harmless prank. The night before, take half a bowl of cereal and put milk over it. Put it into the freezer. In the morning, take the bowl out, cover it the rest of the way with more cereal and milk, and serve!

OOOOO, YUCK!

Wet your hand with water, pretend to sneeze, and sprinkle the water on someone. Here's another gross one: Look at your friend and say, "Oh my gosh! What's that hanging out of your nose?"

COOL DRINKS

Dissolve a package of flavored gelatin according to the directions on the box. Pour the liquid gelatin into drinking glasses, and place a plastic straw in each. Set the glasses on a tray in the refrigerator until the gelatin firms up. Serve the cool beverages to your friends or family … watch them try to drink 'em up!

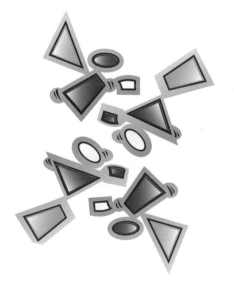

CONFETTI SHOWER

Make confetti by tearing scrap paper into very small pieces. Place confetti into someone's umbrella and then close it and wait for the next rain. Or put the confetti in a coffee mug and pretend to trip, spilling the coffee on an unsuspecting victim. Be a good sport and clean up your mess!

Recipes

 SWAMP CHOMP

Your friends will love making and eating this slimy dessert!

Ingredients:
- Green gelatin
- Bowls or plastic containers
- Gummy bug candy
  (worms, ants, etc.)

Follow the package directions to make green gelatin. Pour some into clear plastic containers and set the rest aside. When the gelatin starts to form, add swarms of gummy bugs. Beat the rest of the gelatin to a froth and add it to the top of the slime. Let set and serve.

 BUG BLOOD

Ask an adult to help you make this creepy beverage for you and your friends.

Ingredients:
- Two 10-oz. packages of frozen strawberries, thawed
- One 6-oz. can of lemonade concentrate, thawed
- One quart of ginger ale
- Two cups of raisins

Mix the strawberries and lemonade concentrate in a blender until smooth and thick. Slowly add ginger ale to the strawberry-lemonade mixture. Pour the drink into a punch bowl, then stir in the raisins and pretend they're tasty "floating bugs!"

 EGG EYEBALLS

So you're not a brain surgeon! How about an eye doctor? You and your friends will have plenty of patients with these eye-popping treats.

Ingredients:
- 6 Eggs, hard-cooked, cooled and peeled
- 6-oz whipped cream cheese
- 12 green olives stuffed with pimentos
- Ketchup
- Toothpick

Ask an adult to hardboil several eggs. When the eggs have cooled, remove the shell, and cut the eggs in half widthwise. Remove the yolks and fill the hole with cream cheese. Press an olive into each cream cheese eyeball, pimento up, for an eerie green iris and red pupil. Dip a toothpick into ketchup and draw broken blood vessels in the cream cheese!

WORMS IN THE MUD

Eat dirt? Eat worms? Sure you can—with this tasty chocolate pudding treat.

Ingredients:

- Instant chocolate pudding mix
- Gummy worms
- Chocolate graham crackers or chocolate sandwich cookies

Follow the directions on the instant pudding package; make sure you stir it enough to get rid of the lumps. Put it in the refrigerator to set. When the pudding is set, crumble up some graham crackers or cookies and mix them into the pudding. Next, stir in some gummy worms, making sure they are covered in pudding. Divide the pudding into four dishes, crumble some more graham crackers on top, and add a couple of worms!

BOOGERS ON A STICK

The name says it all! Kids will love them!

Ingredients:

- 8-ounce jar of processed cheese spread
- 3 or 4 drops green food coloring
- 3 dozen pretzel sticks

Ask an adult to melt the processed cheese spread in the microwave according to jar directions. Allow the cheese to cool slightly in the jar. Carefully stir in green food coloring, using just enough to turn the cheese a pale, snot green color. To form boogers, dip and twist the tip of each pretzel stick into the cheese, lift out, wait twenty seconds, then dip again. When the cheese lumps reach a boogerish size, set boogered pretzels on wax paper to cool.

SEWER SLURPIES

Disgusting? Yes, but tasty too! You and your friends can cool off some with this sweet-tasting ice cream beverage!

Ingredients:
- Chocolate chip ice cream
- Chocolate syrup
- Club soda

Let the ice cream sit at room temperature until it's easy to scoop. Fill tall glasses halfway with the ice cream goop. Squeeze several tablespoons of chocolate syrup into each glass. Slowly fill glasses with club soda and serve with a straw and long spoon.

ADULT SLIME JUICE

Ingredients:
- 6-oz. package of blue powdered drink mix
- 12-oz. can orange juice concentrate
- 1-gallon water

Mix together the orange juice and powdered drink mix, add water, stir and watch the beverage turn green.

Here is another tasty disgusting option:

Ingredients:
- 2 packages of lime gelatin (3 oz. size)
- 1-1/4 cup water, boiling
- 6-oz frozen limeade
- 2 cups water
- Green food coloring
- 10oz Club soda or carbonated water

Ask an adult to prepare the lime gelatin according to the package directions. Carefully pour the mixture into a 9-inch square pan and chill about three hours, until firm. In a large pitcher, combine the limeade, remaining water and food coloring to turn the drink bright green. Chill the drink.

When the gelatin is set, cut out strips or small shapes using cookie cutters.

To serve, add club soda or carbonated water to the limeade and pour over ice. Put a lime gelatin shape in each glass.

GROSS SONGS
and annoying · *kids love to sing!*

STRAWBERRY RETCH

Not much tastes better than a tall, cool glass of Strawberry Retch on a hot, summer day.

Ingredients:
- 3-oz package strawberry gelatin
- 40 ice cubes
- 2 cans of strawberry soda

Ask an adult to prepare the strawberry gelatin according to the package directions. Pour the gelatin into a shallow pan and chill about three hours. When set, make as many cuts as possible across the length and width of the gelatin, forming tiny cubes. Set the gelatin aside. Next, with an adult's help, crush ice cubes in a blender. Spoon alternating layers of crushed ice and gelatin pieces into tall glasses, filling them about 2" away from tops. Slowly pour strawberry soda into each glass until full and stir gently. Serve Strawberry Retch with long spoons and straws.

HOMEMADE ROCK CANDY

With patience you and your friends will have a great sugary sweet treat!

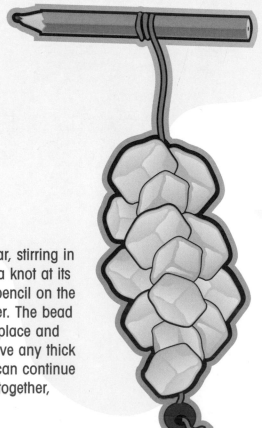

You'll need:
- Clear glass jars
- Hot water
- Granulated sugar
- String
- Bead
- Pencil

Fill a clear glass jar with hot water and dissolve granulated sugar, stirring in one spoonful at a time. Thread a string through a bead and tie a knot at its end; wrap the other end of the string around a pencil. Rest the pencil on the mouth of the jar and allow the bead to dangle in the sugar water. The bead should not touch the bottom of the jar. Place the jar in a warm place and let the sugar water stand undisturbed for a week or more. Remove any thick crust of sugar crystals on the top of the water so that the water can continue to evaporate. As the water evaporates, sugar atoms draw close together, forming cube-shaped sugar crystals. You've made rock candy!

Recipes

ADULT BARF DIP

Ingredients:

- Processed cheese spread
- Tomatoes
- Drained canned corn
- Green onions
- Olives
- Black beans

In a microwave-safe bowl, mash 1/2 can of black beans. Add a small jar of processed cheese spread or cheese dip, some diced tomatoes, drained canned corn, green onions, a few chopped black olives, or any other ugly looking foods. Heat the mixture in the microwave for two or three minutes, stirring frequently. Serve the barf dip with tortilla chips or cut veggies.

BLOODY DESSERT

Ingredients:

- 1/2 cup light corn syrup
- 2 tablespoons creamy peanut butter
- 2 tablespoons chocolate syrup
- Red food coloring

In a small mixing bowl, carefully blend together 1/2 cup light corn syrup, 2 tablespoons of creamy peanut butter, and 2 tablespoons of chocolate syrup. When you have a creamy, smooth mixture stir in 20 or so drops of red food coloring. Smear it on your arm or hand and lick it off! Be careful…this fake blood will stain clothing, carpet, and other surfaces.

CHOCOLATE COVERED BUGS

Ingredients:

- Red-licorice whips
- Soft caramel candies
- Chocolate chips
- Optional: colored sprinkles, candies, coconut, sliced almonds

Wash your hands before making these delicious sweet tasting chocolate bugs. First, cut the licorice whips into small pieces and set them aside. Unwrap the caramels and flatten each one into a small oval. Press the small pieces of licorice onto each flattened caramel to make bug legs. Top each bug with a second caramel and seal together by pressing the edges. Put each bug on a baking sheet lined with waxed paper.

With adult help, melt the chocolate chips in a microwave-safe bowl. Microwave on High about 1 minute. Stir. Then microwave on High 1 minute longer. Remove the chocolate from the microwave and stir until melted. Spoon melted chocolate over each caramel. Decorate the bugs with nuts, candies, coconut, or sprinkles.

 ## SPIDER GUTS

Slice into this gooey cake for a disgusting surprise!

Ingredients:
- 1 Basic cake mix
- 1 Package of green gelatin, prepared according to package directions
- Black frosting—available at craft supply stores or make your own by adding blue food coloring to chocolate frosting
- Black licorice sticks or whips
- Large green gumdrops

Mix the cake batter according to package directions. Ask an adult to bake the cake in a bowl. Once the cake has baked and cooled, remove it from the mold. To make the spider's body, cut the cake in half horizontally. Scoop out a hole in each half. Fill the hole with the green gelatin. Put both halves of the cake back together. Frost it black and arrange on a serving platter. Add licorice whip legs, gumdrop eyes, and candy body markings. When the cake is cut into, it will ooze green guts!

 ## BRAIN FOOD

Your friends might come to believe you're a brain surgeon after enjoying this tasty treat.

You'll need:
- Several packages of lime gelatin
- One 16-oz. can of fruit cocktail or 1-1/2 cups of grated carrots

Ask an adult to prepare the gelatin by following the directions on the package. Pour the liquid gelatin into a dome-shaped mold or mixing bowl. When the gelatin is half-set, drain the fruit cocktail and add it to the gelatin. Use carrots, too. Allow the gelatin to chill and completely set. Carefully flip the mold and place the gelatin on a platter.

Cross

Recipes

CHOPPED OFF FINGERS PIZZA

ADULT

Make the next homemade pizza one to remember with these misplaced fingertips.

Ingredients:

- 1 Red bell pepper
- Mozzarella sticks
- Baked pizza crusts
- Pizza sauce

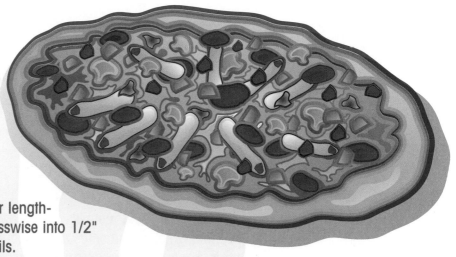

Core, stem and seed, and cut a red pepper lengthwise into 1" wide strips. Cut each strip crosswise into 1/2" pieces. Trim one end to make the fingernails.

Make fingers by cutting each cheese stick in half crosswise. Cut out a 1/2" square notch on the rounded end of each "finger" into which a pepper piece will fit to make a fingernail.

Prepare your homemade pizza crust, sauce, and toppings. Lay several cheese fingers well apart on the crust. Place a red pepper fingernail onto each. Bake as directed.

WORM BURGERS

ADULT

These aged, wormy burgers are certain to get a reaction from unsuspecting dinner guests!

Ingredients:

- 1-1/2 cup bean sprouts
- 1 lb Ground beef
- 1 Egg
- Salt and pepper to taste
- Mayonnaise, ketchup, mustard
- Hamburger buns

First, wash your hands—nobody wants dirt mixed into their wormy burgers! Now, wash the bean sprouts with warm water. Mix 1 cup of bean sprouts, ground beef and raw egg together in a bowl. Save the remaining sprouts until later. With adult help, form the burgers into patties, season, and cook them as usual. When they're cooked through, place each on an open bun and sprinkle the remaining "worms" on top. Don't forget the pus and blood on the side—ketchup, mustard, mayonnaise mixed together!

Instructions for Play:

MEMORY MATCH

Place all cards face down on the table. The object of the game is for a player to collect pairs of cards, matching content and color. To play, players flip two cards at a time. If the cards match content and color, the player removes the pair, sets them aside, and tries to find another matching pair. If the cards do not match, flip the cards face down and it becomes the next player's turn. If a player flips over the spoon, the player flips the spoon face down and rearranges all the remaining cards in play. Play continues until all the cards are removed. The player with the most pairs is the winner.

NOT ME WITHOUT A SPOON! 1

"Great big globs of greasy grimy gopher guts…and me without a spoon!" In this twist on Old Maid, the player WITH the spoon at the end is the winner. Deal all the cards to the players. Each player looks at the cards in their hand and places any pairs face up in front of them. Players take turns drawing a card from another player's hand, and placing any pairs on the table.

NOT ME WITHOUT A SPOON! 2

Place the spoon card face up in the center of the table. The object of the game is to grab the spoon card after you have collected all the cards of one kind. To play, deal all of the cards to the players. A player offers to trade 1, 2, or 3 cards he or she does not want, in hopes of getting cards of the kind he or she is collecting. Do not say what cards you are collecting. Do not show the cards in trading; keep them face-side down. Simply say, "Trade one, one, one," or "Trade two, two, two," or "Trade three, three, three." All players trade simultaneously—there are no turns! The player who has collected all eight cards quietly grabs the spoon card from the center.

GO FISH!

Deal all of the cards to the players, plus one additional pile—the fishing pool. When all of the players have laid down all of the pairs that they have, the game begins. The first player asks the player to their left for a specific card. In order to ask for a card, you must be holding one of that same content and color. If the person has the card that you asked for, take the card and lay your pair face up on the table. Your turn continues. If the person doesn't have the card that you asked for, then you are told to "Go fish!" and must draw a card from the fishing pool. If you draw the card that you were asking for, you can continue your turn. If you don't draw the card you need, then it is the next person's turn. The game continues until one player has no cards left in their hand.